Keep this pocket-sized Frith book with you when you are travelling around Dartmoor.

Whether you are in your car or on foot, you will enjoy an evocative journey back in time. Compare the Dartmoor of old with what you can see today —see how the landscapes of the moor have changed, how its buildings and beauty spots have been altered and developed, look at the monuments and antiquities as our ancestors saw them. See the many alterations to Dartmoor that have taken place during our lives, and which we may have taken for granted.

At the turn of a page you will gain fascinating insights into Dartmoor's unique history.

D1341534

FRANCIS *FRITH'S*
pocket ALBUM

DARTMOOR

A POCKET ALBUM

Adapted from an original book by
MARTIN DUNNING

FRITH
BOOK Co

First published in the United Kingdom in 2003 by
Frith Book Company Ltd

ISBN 1-85937-710-6

British Library Cataloguing in Publication Data

Dartmoor—A Pocket Album
Adapted from an original book by Martin Dunning

Frith Book Company Ltd
Frith's Barn, Teffont,
Salisbury, Wiltshire SP3 5QP
Tel: +44 (0) 1722 716 376
Email: info@francisfrith.co.uk
www.francisfrith.co.uk

Printed and bound in Great Britain by MPG, Bodmin

Front Cover: Haytor, the Rocks 1927 / 79777 *The colour-tinting is for
illustrative purposes only, and is not intended to be historically accurate.*

Frontispiece: Lustleigh, The Village 1907 / 58444

CONTENTS

FRANCIS FRITH
VICTORIAN PIONEER

Francis Frith, founder of the world-famous photographic archive, was a complex and multi-talented man. A devout Quaker and a highly successful Victorian businessman, he was philosophic by nature and pioneering in outlook. By 1855 he had already established a wholesale grocery business in Liverpool, and sold it for the astonishing sum of £200,000, which is the equivalent today of over £15,000,000. Now in his thirties, and captivated by the new science of photography, Frith set out on a series of pioneering journeys up the Nile and to the Near East.

INTRIGUE AND EXPLORATION

He was the first photographer to venture beyond the sixth cataract of the Nile. Africa was still the mysterious 'Dark Continent', and Stanley and Livingstone's historic meeting was a decade into the future. The conditions for picture taking confound belief. He laboured for hours in his wicker dark-room in the sweltering heat of the desert, while the volatile chemicals fizzed dangerously in their trays. Back in London he exhibited his photographs and was 'rapturously cheered' by members of the Royal Society. His reputation as a photographer was made overnight.

VENTURE OF A LIFE-TIME

By the 1870s the railways had threaded their way across the country, and Bank Holidays and half-day Saturdays had been made obligatory by Act of Parliament. All of a sudden the working man and his family were able to enjoy days out, take holidays, and see a little more of the world.

With typical business acumen, Francis Frith foresaw that these new tourists would enjoy having souvenirs to commemorate their days out. For the next thirty years he travelled the country by train and by pony and trap, producing fine photographs of seaside resorts and beauty spots that were keenly bought by millions of Victorians. These prints were painstakingly pasted into family albums and pored over during the dark nights of winter, rekindling precious memories of summer excursions. Frith's studio was soon supplying retail shops all over the country, and by 1890 F Frith & Co had become the greatest specialist photographic publishing company in the world, with over 2,000 sales outlets, and pioneered the picture postcard.

FRANCIS FRITH'S LEGACY

Francis Frith had died in 1898 at his villa in Cannes, his great project still growing. The archive he created continued in business for another seventy years. By 1970 it contained over a third of a million pictures showing 7,000 British towns and villages.

Frith's legacy to us today is of immense significance and value, for the magnificent archive of evocative photographs he created provides a unique record of change in the cities, towns and villages throughout Britain over a century and more. Frith and his fellow studio photographers revisited locations many times down the years to update their views, compiling for us an enthralling and colourful pageant of British life and character.

We are fortunate that Frith was dedicated to recording the minutiae of everyday life. For it is this sheer wealth of visual data, the painstaking chronicle of changes in dress, transport, street layouts, buildings, housing, engineering and landscape that captivates us so much today, offering us a powerful link with the past and with the lives of our ancestors.

Computers have now made it possible for Frith's many thousands of images to be accessed almost instantly. The archive offers every one of us an opportunity to examine the places where we and our families have lived and worked down the years. Its images, depicting our shared past, are now bringing pleasure and enlightenment to millions around the world a century and more after his death.

CHAGFORD, OLD HOUSE 1907 / 58472

DARTMOOR
THE GRANITE HEART OF DEVON

SIT ATOP one of the high tors on a summer afternoon—Great Mis Tor, say, north of the B3357 that runs from Princetown to Tavistock. It has taken getting on for half an hour to reach the summit, for although the distance is only just over a mile the hillside climbs over 500 feet to reach the jumble of granite that makes up the tor. It has been time and distance enough to flush the city out of both lungs and mind.

Here, 1765 feet above sea level in the bleached blue of an August sky, it is possible to see many of Dartmoor's faces. North and east lie the high moors— ridges and plateaux of bleak grassland and bog fading into the distance, dotted here and there with sheep and with the dark sentinel of Fur

Tor standing mysterious and lonely five miles away. The River Walkham, here little more than a brook, jinks its way through the valley past the remains of a bronze age village, visible now only in the outline of its fields and hut circles.

South-east is Princetown, hidden behind the rounded bulk of North Hessary Tor with its intrusive television mast; to the west the moors drop away to a patchwork of fields and Tavistock, nestling in the Tavy valley. South of Great Mis the Walkham continues past the ugly scar of Merrivale Quarry and drops into a deep, thickly-wooded valley on its way to join the Tavy, the Tamar, and eventually the sea.

Dartmoor's rivers radiate out from the great central plateau like the spokes of a wheel. They start as little more than wet, boggy patches which feed small streams flowing through shallow valleys, but when they reach the edge of the plateau they race off, cutting the deep and winding valleys that are so characteristic of the perimeter of the moor. South and west run the Walkham, the Tavy, the Plym and the Erme. To the north the Taw and Torridge head off through the farmlands of North Devon towards the Bristol Channel, the Teign skirts the north-east corner of the moor, and the eastern part of Dartmoor is drained by the Dart and its tributaries.

The high moors are a harsh environment, supporting little save sheep and ravens, and so the sheltered valleys hold most of Dartmoor's settlements. There are busy market towns such as Tavistock, Moretonhampstead and Ashburton—towns which were founded on the proceeds of tin mined on the hills. And there are the villages. The great Dartmoor writer William Crossing wrote a series of articles, later published in book form, entitled 'Gems in a Granite Setting', a phrase that could hardly be bettered as a description of places like Widecombe, Lustleigh and Buckland in the Moor. Snug in their valleys, surrounded by a patchwork of fields or peeping coyly from oak woodlands, the subject of a thousand postcards and millions of holiday snaps, Dartmoor's villages are saved from being chocolate-box and twee by their functionality. True, the thatched roofs of Ponsford and the mellow granite walls dusted with the grey-green and golden lichen of centuries look great on a postcard and would make wonderful locations for a film, but little settlements like this have evolved as a practical response to the landscape in which they lie—a granite landscape, and granite is too stern a medium to allow for ostentation and frippery. The beauty of granite is better expressed in the simple lines of a farmhouse than the grandeur of a mansion.

Granite is the heart of the moor—literally. Millions of years ago, a great bubble of molten rock pushed its way up through the earth's crust and crystallised as granite. Over the millennia, the softer overlying rocks were eroded away, leaving the huge dome of Dartmoor standing proud and reaching over 2,000 feet in the north. The granite is covered with peaty, acid soils and only breaks through the surface in the form of tors—massive blocks, weathered into curious and exotic shapes. Some of the tors are surrounded by clitter slopes, jumbles of granite blocks strewn on the hillside, which would have been the only source of stone for the earliest inhabitants of the moor.

During the Neolithic and Bronze Ages, between 5,000 and 500 BC, the climate was kinder than it is today, and man was able to colonise the high moors. He built enclosures for his animals, huts for himself, tombs for his ancestors and stone rows and megaliths, presumably for the gods. The remains of early man's efforts are to be seen all over the moor: Grimspound is one of the best examples of a Bronze Age settlement in Europe, while Spinster's Rock near Chagford is a magnificent Neolithic Dolmen or burial chamber. The stone rows of Merrivale and Down Tor, with their imposing megaliths, are something of a mystery—were they of astrological or religious significance? No matter—touch them and feel history under your fingertips.

Man came down from the moors at some stage and began to build his settlements in the valleys, but he still ventured out onto the heights to tend his flocks and to travel, and here again he used granite. The ancient crosses that loom out of the mist are often landmarks on the routes that traversed the moor, such as the Abbot's Way which linked the great abbeys at Buckfast and Tavistock. In addition to its use for building, Dartmoor's granite held other, more hidden riches. As the rock cooled it released vapours of various metals which condensed to form veins of ore. There were exotic metals such as tungsten, silver, arsenic and even uranium, there were copper, lead and iron—and there was tin.

Mining for tin, and later copper, was to bring something of an industrial boom to Dartmoor. Tin was worked in three phases: in early medieval times, when Plympton was a great tin port before the waste silted up the estuary, and when Chagford, Ashburton and Tavistock became Stannary Towns, allowing them to test and stamp tin; the Elizabethan period, when such luminaries as Sir Walter Raleigh held the title of Lord Warden of the Stannaries; and the Victorian boom, which saw huge quantities of ore transported along the Tavistock Canal to the River Tamar.

PRINCETOWN THE SQUARE c1955 / P115001

DARTMOOR THE PONIES c1965 / D6135

Dartmoor was plundered for its mineral wealth. In the south, huge pits were dug for china clay, an industry that continues today, and all over the moor granite was quarried for building stone. Tor Royal and Foggintor provided stone for the building of the prison, while King's Tor and Swell Tor quarries produced the corbel stones for London Bridge, some of which can be seen, unused, near the old Princetown railway line.

The advent of the railways gave hitherto isolated towns a link with the outside world. By the beginning of the 20th century, Tavistock, Lydford and Okehampton in the west had stations, and in the east Bovey Tracey, Lustleigh and Moretonhampstead all benefited from the construction of the Teign Valley line. However, communities away from the railways were still dependent on the horse, and it was not until the arrival of the motor car that Dartmoor's last great industry took off.

Tourism is Dartmoor's lifeblood today. Widecombe, Haytor, Dartmeet, Princetown—they all play host to coachfuls of day trippers; on a busy summer Sunday the roads are crammed with cars, the occupants of which rarely stray more than a hundred yards from the safety of tarmac. Postcards are sold, probably in millions, cream teas scoffed, and the pubs do a thriving lunchtime trade.

Move away from the main roads and the tourist honeypots, however, or visit the moor in winter, and a different picture emerges. Dartmoor is not merely a leisure facility; it is a living, vital land where woodlands have to be managed, dry stone walls repaired, lambing attended to and ponies and cattle rounded up. The endless cycle of life continues through the seasons and whatever the weather, for the people of the moor are not allowed the luxury of seeing it only when the sun shines. The high moor has over a hundred inches of rain a year, and Plymouth, a mere fifteen miles south of Princetown, can be basking in sunshine when the tops are shrouded in a mist that can reduce visibility to twenty yards. Snowfall and high winds can render the moor almost arctic, and while the truly great blizzards are not as common as they once were, memories persist of the vicious winters of 1947 and 1963 when farms and villages were cut off and snow lay on the ground for months.

Back at Great Mis Tor, on this shimmering summer day, winter seems unimaginable. Far towards the southern horizon the Eddystone lighthouse sits on a gunmetal sea, and to the north the blue of the Bristol Channel is just visible over the Cornish fields. A farmer, aided by four darting, crouching collies, drives a flock of sheep across the northern slope of the tor. Above, a skylark sings exuberantly as he flies, and a pair of buzzards soar, quartering the hillside in search of rabbits. Sunlight glints off the windscreen of a car as it crosses Merrivale Bridge; but here at the summit, 800 feet above the road, it seems that the 21st century has barely touched this vast and ancient landscape.

IVYBRIDGE

GENERAL VIEW *1890 / 22517*

There was a chapel in Ivybridge from 1402, but the modern Church of St John was not built until 1882. Ivybridge did not become a parish until 1894, taking parts of the parishes of Ugborough and Ermington.

IVYBRIDGE

THE OLD CHURCH 1890 / 22522

The 13th-century bridge spanning the River Erme was built as a result of the increase in traffic that occurred because of the growth of nearby Plymouth. The Erme reaches the sea at Mothecombe.

IVYBRIDGE

THE BRIDGE c1955 / I22043

Today the town of Iybridge has grown enormously and acts mainly as a dormitory for Plymouth, but it was once a busy market town; this paper mill on the bank of the Erme was a major employer.

IVYBRIDGE
FROM THE RIVER c1866 / 8304

PLYM BRIDGE

THE BRIDGE AND THE RIVER 1925 / 78417

Plym Bridge now lies several miles inland from the estuary, but at one time the tide reached the bridge. Centuries of silting caused by waste from tin mines on the moor were to blame.

SOUTH BRENT

CHURCH STREET c1955 / S360003

South Brent, on the River Avon, has a beautiful 15th-century church, St Petroc's, which has the unusual distinction of being the only church in the country apart from Canterbury Cathedral to have had its priest murdered in the church. John Hay was dragged from the sanctuary and beaten to death by Thomas Wake.

Dartmoor's clapper bridges, despite their prehistoric look, are actually medieval; they were constructed for the packhorse trains that were the transport system of the moor. The giant slabs that make up the spans can weigh up to eight tons.

POSTBRIDGE

THE CLAPPER BRIDGE 1907 / 5788

Postbridge takes its name from the arched bridge that was built to carry the post road from Princetown in the south-west to Moretonhampstead in the north-east. The bridges span the East Dart River, which rises near Whitehorse Hill on the high moors in the distance.

POSTBRIDGE

THE VILLAGE 1931 / 83921

The origins of the Judges Chair, sometimes called the Druids Chair (although there were no druids on the moor), are vague. One story is that it was made from slabs taken from the old Stannary Parliament at Crockern Tor, three miles away.

DUNNABRIDGE

THE JUDGES CHAIR 1910 / 62315

Dartmeet lies on an old packhorse route, which was also used by miners from Ashburton and the east of the moor to attend the Stannary Parliament which sat at Crockern Tor just north of Two Bridges.

DARTMEET

THE BRIDGE AND COTTAGE c1871 / 5530

A mile uphill from the bridge on the road to Ashburton is the Coffin Stone, a resting place for coffin bearers on the long walk to the church at Widecombe where funerals took place. The stone is said to have been split in half by lightning when the coffin of an evil man was rested there.

DARTMEET

GENERAL VIEW 1925 / 78513

DARTMEET

THE RIVER DART 1890 / 25948

Dartmeet is at the confluence of the East Dart, just visible at centre left, and the West Dart. The buildings of the small hamlet remain, but the thatched house on the right has been altered greatly and now has a slate roof.

The Upper Dart flows through a magnificent wooded valley over looked by rugged outcrops such as Ausewell Rocks (just visible through the trees on the right), Bench Tor, Luckey Tor and Eagle Rock.

THE UPPER DART

VIEW FROM UPPER BUCKLAND DRIVE 1890 / 25961

New Bridge is the starting point for canoeists embarking on the stretch of the river known as 'The Loop'—a three-mile whitewater run downstream to Holne Bridge, tackled in winter when the river is in spate.

THE RIVER DART

NEW BRIDGE 1890 / 25954

Widecombe, probably Dartmoor's most well-known village, stands in the broad valley ('Wide Combe') of the East Webburn river. Its famous fair takes place in Old Field on the second Tuesday in September. The first recorded fair was a cattle fair held in 1850.

WIDECOMBE IN THE MOOR

GENERAL VIEW c1955 / W95038

WIDECOMBE IN THE MOOR

YE OLD FORGE c1955 / W95012

Although surrounded by a patchwork of fields, Widecombe is a real moorland village, and the skyline is dominated by the tors: centre right is Bonehill Rocks, to the left is Bell Tor and on the far left the bump on the skyline is Chinkwell Tor.

WIDECOMBE IN THE MOOR

AT THE VILLAGE SIGN 1927 / 79793

This view looks west from somewhere near Bonehill Rocks. The ridge beyond Widecombe leads right out of the picture to Hamel Down and forms part of the Two Moors Way, which links Dartmoor and Exmoor.

WIDECOMBE IN THE MOOR

FROM THE MOORS c1965 / D6101

Widecombe is an enormous parish—some 11,000 acres—and local people travel for miles to worship at the Church of St Pancras, which has become known as 'The Cathedral of the Moors'. In 1638 a thunderbolt hit the church, killing four worshippers and injuring sixty-two.

WIDECOMBE IN THE MOOR

THE CHURCH TOWER 1907 / 5805

Haytor Rocks stand on one side of a broad grassy avenue. Opposite is Low Man, the west face of which is the highest cliff on the moor at 130 feet. One local claims that in the winter of 1963 the snowdrifts at Low Man were so deep he tobogganed off the top! This is a favourite spot today for tourists because of its height (457 metres) and the panoramic views as far as Portland in the east and The Lizard in the south-west. In the 19th century Haytor was more likely to be frequented by quarrymen working the granite quarries on the other side of the hill.

HAYTOR
THE ROCKS

1927 / 79779A

HAYTOR
THE ROCKS 1927 / 79777

The Rock Hotel still stands in the village of Haytor Vale, providing refreshment for tourists just as it once did for the local writer and eccentric Beatrice Chase. The author of many romantic works about the moor, she took the title of 'My Lady of the Moor' bestowed on her by an admirer.

HAYTOR

THE ROCK HOTEL 1931 / 83928

HAYTOR

MOORLAND ROAD TO WIDECOMBE

1920 / 69622

There used to be several of these improbably-balanced natural rock formations on the moor. They could be rocked to and fro quite easily, and this one was known as the Nutcracker, for obvious reasons. It fell prey to vandals.

RIPPON TOR
THE LOGAN STONE c1871 / 5799

Hiding in the valley of the West Webburn River, which eventually joins the East Webburn and flows into the Dart, Ponsworthy is one of the moor's most attractive hamlets. The Splash is a ford where a tributary stream flows over the road.

PONSWORTHY

THE SPLASH c1960 / D6142

Grimspound, a few miles north of the village of Widecombe, is one of the finest examples of a Bronze Age village in Europe. It lies half a mile off the road to the right. On the horizon is Hookney Tor.

GRIMSPOUND

1922 / 73161

The 15th-century bridge at Holne spans a deep pool in the river, and has become a very popular spot for the time-honoured pastime of bridge-jumping, usually undertaken after some minutes spent teetering on the parapet with pulse racing!

THE RIVER DART

HOLNE BRIDGE 1890 / 25949

BUCKFASTLEIGH

THE ABBEY c1965 / B238047

Buckfastleigh sits at the edge of the moor, surrounded by low, steep hills. It was still a village in the 19th century, but a busy one: it was the centre for considerable industrial activity, with four blanket and serge mills employing several hundred workers. The tradition of woollen manufacturing in Buckfastleigh was ancient, for the Cistercian monks here were wool traders, and transported their cloth along the old Abbot's Way, a green path that crossed the moors to Plymouth.

BUCKFASTLEIGH

FORE STREET 1952 / B238016

BUCKFASTLEIGH

ST MARY'S ABBEY 1922 / 73191

Buckfastleigh's ancient abbey was a ruin in the 19th century, and there is little left of the original building complex other than an old barn and a tower. However, in 1906 the monks embarked on an ambitious project to rebuild an abbey here using only their own labour. Never more than six monks were working at any time, and most had to learn their skills almost overnight. By 1922 the building was two-thirds finished and was officially opened.

50

There are records of bull baiting in Ashburton as far back as 1174. It was made illegal in 1835, by which time locals could seek their entertainment in one of the town's many pubs, such as the Royal Oak, which is still open for business today.

ASHBURTON

EAST STREET AND THE BULL RING 1922 / 73181

ASHBURTON

NORTH STREET 1904 / 51203

Ashburton lies on the River Ashburn, and was declared a Stannary Town in 1285 by Edward I. This allowed the official testing and stamping of tin, which contributed greatly to the town's wealth and also to the exchequer through Coinage Duty.

ASHBURTON

NORTH STREET 1890 / 25944

Some of the kerbstones which line Ashburton's narrow streets are made from fine pink marble, quarried locally. At one point they were nearly removed during a road improvement scheme, but prompt action by the locals preserved them.

ASHBURTON

NORTH STREET 1922 / 73180

The market town of Bovey Tracey at one time had two railway stations; now it has none. The Dolphin Hotel is an old coaching and posting house. By 1907 the railways had reduced reliance on coaches, and this one is probably an excursion coach.

BOVEY TRACEY

THE COACH FOR THE MOORS 1907 / 58522

Lustleigh Cleave, one of the Moor's most scenic valleys, lies to the west of Lustleigh itself and was cut by the River Bovey. This view is probably from Sharpitor, one of the many rocky outcrops that dot the northern side of the Cleave.

LUSTLEIGH CLEAVE

FROM THE EAST c1871 / 5811

LUSTLEIGH

THE VILLAGE 1907 / 58444

LUSTLEIGH

THE VILLAGE 1907 / 58446

Lustleigh is a showpiece still of the thatcher's art. West country thatching is done with straw, rather than the reed that is used in other parts of the country, but the tools are much the same— iron hooks, hand shears, shearing hook, sparhook and leggat.

LUSTLEIGH

AN OLD COTTAGE 1906 / 56596

LUSTLEIGH

FROM THE EAST 1920 / 69626

This is an idyllic scene—horses no longer work the land now, but as late as 1987 they were being used by the National Park Authority in woodlands near Moretonhampstead. Just visible in the centre of the picture is the Teign Valley railway line, which used to run alongside the moor to Moretonhampstead.

The Church of St John the Baptist's most eccentric incumbent was the Rev William Davy (1743-1826), who printed twenty-six volumes of his 'System of Divinity' (unreadable, apparently, although you are welcome to try if you can find a copy) and followed it up with a mere six volumes of collected sermons. Neither made the best-seller list.

LUSTLEIGH
THE VILLAGE c1960 / L115027

BECKY FALLS

1922 / 73158

MANATON

VIEW ON THE OLD MANATON ROAD 1907 / 58459

Manaton is on the valley side above Hayne Brook, which joins the Bovey via Becka Brook. Milk churns such as those here are no longer seen—milk is now collected by tanker.

MANATON

THE MOORS c1955 / M20016

This was the scene of a devastating lightning strike on 13 December 1779. The east front of the chancel was demolished (perhaps explaining the new roof tiles on the right) and the north side of the tower was split almost to the ground. 'In short a sight shocking to all beholders' (Manaton Parish Register).

MANATON

THE CHURCH 1907 / 58460

MORETONHAMPSTEAD

GENERAL VIEW 1931 / 84050

Moretonhampstead stands on the watershed between the Teign and Bovey Rivers. In the Domesday Book its name is recorded as Mortona, and it was later known as Mor Tun; locals still refer to it as Moreton. Prominent on the horizon (right) are Haytor and Low Man.

MORETONHAMPSTEAD

The Sentry is the name given to the hillside in front of the church, which commands good views of the southern approaches to Moretonhampstead. Stooks of corn like those in this picture have long faded into countryside memory.

MORETON-
HAMPSTEAD

THE SENTRY 1918 / 68599

The Church of St Andrew, with its fine Gothic granite tower, dates from around 1418. On the right a wheelwright is going about his trade.

MORETONHAMPSTEAD

CHURCH STREET 1906 / 56604

The White Hart Hotel was the venue for the last Stannary Parliament to be held on Dartmoor on 11 December 1786. The practice of holding the Parliament at Crockern Tor, 1,200 feet up in the middle of the moor, had very sensibly ceased some time before.

MORETONHAMPSTEAD

CROSS STREET c1960 / M97012

Fingle Bridge, typical of an old Dartmoor pack bridge, spans the River Teign. On the right is The Angler's Rest and behind it Prestonbury Hill, on top of which is the prehistoric Prestonbury Fort.

DREWSTEIGNTON

FINGLE BRIDGE c1960 / D85011

The Teign is a great sea trout river, much fished by the likes of the Reverend Richard Peak, a 19th-century Rector of Drewsteignton who spent as much time casting the fly as he did looking after his flock.

DREWSTEIGNTON

FINGLE BRIDGE c1960 / D85001

The Church of the Holy Trinity was built in the 15th and 16th centuries, and the chancel was rebuilt in 1863. On the left is the Drew Arms, which had one of the longest-serving landladies in the country—Aunt Mabel Mudge, who held the licence for over 60 years.

DREWSTEIGNTON

THE CHURCH c1960 / D85002

This photograph was taken from the eastern end of the glen, two miles upstream from Fingle Bridge. The cliff in the centre is Sharp Tor which, unusually for Dartmoor, is shale rather than granite.

FINGLE GLEN

VIEW OVER THE RIVER TEIGN 1910 / 62444

Chagford's striking octagonal Market House was built in 1862. An earlier Market House collapsed in 1618, killing ten people who were attending the Stannary Court. Chagford was declared one of the first Devon Stannary towns in 1305, but by the late 16th century the tin was worked out and the town turned to spinning wool.

CHAGFORD

MARKET PLACE 1906 / 56609

CHAGFORD

RUSHFORD BRIDGE 1907 / 58475

The porch of the Three Crowns was the scene in 1643 of the shooting during a skirmish with Parliamentarian forces of the Royalist poet Sidney Godolphin, described by a contemporary as 'perfect and as absolute a piece of virtue as ever our nation bred'.

CHAGFORD

THE THREE CROWNS 1922 / 73126

84

Mill Street is named after the blanket and serge mill opened in the early 18th century by a Mr Berry, whose town house is now the Moorlands Hotel.

CHAGFORD

MILL STREET 1922 / 73125A

The Globe Hotel was originally a post house. The London and South Western Railway used to pick up here for Exeter railway station.

CHAGFORD

THE GLOBE HOTEL 1931 / 83907

The Town Hall (left) was built in 1685 by John Northmore as a private house and converted in 1821. Okehampton received its charter in 1623 and until 1832 sent two MPs to Parliament.

OKEHAMPTON

FORE STREET MARKET 1890 / 22590

The main church of Okehampton is a little way out of town;
the one in this picture is the Chantry Chapel of St James. The
tower was built in the 15th century, and the rest was rebuilt in
1862.

OKEHAMPTON

FORE STREET c1871 / 5765

OKEHAMPTON

FORE STREET 1906 / 56049

Okehampton is remembered by many people as the scene of holiday traffic jams on the A30. Sparke's butchers was demolished in the 1930s for road widening, but traffic remained a nightmare until the bypass was opened in 1985. The White Hart Hotel is still open.

The viaduct was built in 1874 over the West Okement River
to carry the Lydford Junction to Okehampton line. It spans
561 feet and is 150 feet high. The upper part of the valley
now holds Meldon Reservoir.

OKEHAMPTON

MELDON VIADUCT 1906 / 56058

Okehampton was founded by Baldwin de Brionne, Norman Sheriff of Devon in 1086. The Norman keep of the castle dates from around that time, and the rest is 13th-century.

OKEHAMPTON

THE CASTLE 1890 / 22589

The River Lyd rises high on the moor near Woodcock Hill and eventually joins the Tamar near Lifton. Lydford was a Saxon Mint Town and a seat of power under Alfred the Great.

LYDFORD

THE RIVER LYD AND BRAT TOR 1922 / 73176

The Castle was built in 1195 to supersede the previous earthworks. The castle dungeon was used as the Stannary Prison, although Lydford never had the status of Stannary Town.

LYDFORD

THE CASTLE 1906 / 56070

In the 17th century, Lydford's famous gorge was home to a gang of red-bearded ruffians called the Gubbins, who terrorised the locals before dying 'as a result of intemperance and interbreeding'.

LYDFORD

THE GORGE c1955 / D6096

This photograph was taken from the tower of the 15th-century church of St Petroc. In the distance rise the westernmost hills of the moor, culminating at the prominent nipple of Yes Tor (2028 feet) just left of centre.

LYDFORD

THE VILLAGE AND THE TORS 1907 / 57508

LYDFORD

The London and South Western Railway arrived from Tavistock in 1865, and the line to Okehampton was completed in 1874. The last train on the line ran on 6 May 1968.

Elliots Hotel became the Bullers Arms before taking the name it has today—The Mary Tavy Inn. Two miles north of Mary Tavy is Wheal Betsy, one of Dartmoor's most famous mines; in the middle of the 19th century it was producing over 1,000 tons of lead and 2,000 ounces of silver annually.

MARY TAVY

ELLIOTS HOTEL 1908 / 59741

Tavistock, one of Devon's three original Stannary Towns, lies on the banks of the Tavy, which rises high on the moors near Cut Hill and flows into the Tamar upstream of Tamerton. In the background is the viaduct of the Okehampton railway line.

TAVISTOCK

GENERAL VIEW 1893 / 32113

TAVISTOCK

DUKE STREET 1910 / 62256

This view looks west. Symon's Jewellers was founded in the 1880s by J E Symons on Duke Street. He opened these premises on West Street in 1904 and eventually moved all his business here.

TAVISTOCK

WEST STREET 1922 / 73204

Construction of the Guildhall was commenced in 1848 on the orders of the 7th Duke, whose statue stands in front. It was completed in 1864. As well as filling the usual civic functions, it was also the Police Station and the home of the fire engine.

TAVISTOCK

THE GUILDHALL 1893 / 32118

The hotel was originally the Abbey House, but was converted to a hotel in 1822. The low building is the Bedford estate office. Tavistock's Goose fair is held in Bedford Square on the second Wednesday in October.

TAVISTOCK

THE BEDFORD HOTEL 1893 / 32120

Abbey Bridge was built in 1763 to carry the turnpike road to Plymouth. It was widened in 1860 to give access to the Great Western Railway station. The weir was destroyed in a flood in 1890 and rebuilt.

TAVISTOCK

ABBEY BRIDGE 1896 / 38914

Merrivale Bridge crosses the Walkham, which rises in the centre of the high moors. This old bridge still stands, but the Princetown to Tavistock road now takes a newer bridge alongside.

MERRIVALE

THE BRIDGE 1910 / 62321

In the background is Merrivale Quarry, granite from which has been used in many famous public buildings including the old London Bridge, now in Arizona. The quarry cottages are long gone, but the Dartmoor Inn (centre) is a popular watering-hole still.

MERRIVALE

THE BRIDGE 1910 / 62319

WALKHAMPTON

HUCKWORTHY BRIDGE 1910 / 62289

HORRABRIDGE

THE BRIDGE 1898 / 42243

There has been a bridge over the Walkham here since the 11th century. Recent roadworks revealed within the existing structure a much earlier bridge, possibly medieval, around which the present bridge was built. Upstream (right) of the bridge is a weir, at which it is possible to see salmon leaping.

HORRABRIDGE

THE BRIDGE 1898 / 42244

This part of Yelverton, separated from the rest of the village by the main road, goes by the curious name of Leg O'Mutton. The Midland Bank, now HSBC, still opens three days a week, and the cafe on the left is now a hairdressers.

YELVERTON

THE VILLAGE c1965 / Y10028

The Yelverton Hotel is now the Leg O'Mutton, and the flat-roofed building beyond is today home to the Walkham Gallery and a haberdashers. The garage is still open, but no longer sells petrol.

YELVERTON

THE HOTEL c1955 / Y10021

YELVERTON

THE PARADE 1934 / 86251

The rocks stand at the end of what was during World War Two the runway of RAF Harrowbeer, so called because of worries that 'RAF Yelverton' might sound too much like 'RAF Yeovilton' on the crackly radio of a Spitfire or Hurricane. The rocks were lowered by several feet to prevent planes flying into them.

YELVERTON

ROBOROUGH ROCKS 1898 / 42255

Princetown is an unlikely spot for a town—1400 feet above sea level, on an exposed col between North Hessary Tor (top left, without the TV mast that adorns it today) and South Hessary Tor, and with a massive annual rainfall of between 80 and 100 inches.

PRINCETOWN

DARTMOOR PRISON 1890 / 22574

The prison regime was harsh; convicts were often harnessed to haul carts, and most spent their time breaking rocks in the quarries in the severe Dartmoor climate. Beatings and floggings were common, and strait-jackets, leg-irons and the ball and chain were all used. Not for nothing was it known as 'Halfway to Hell'.

PRINCETOWN

DARTMOOR PRISON GATE AND CONVICTS 1890 / 22578

A somewhat macabre tourist industry sprung up around the prison, with charabancs bringing people from far and wide to gawp at 7 Tor View, Princetown - the prison's postal address.

PRINCETOWN

TAVISTOCK ROAD 1931 / 84058

THE WARREN HOUSE INN

1931 / 84044

The Warren House Inn, at over 1400 feet above sea level, has the distinction of being the highest pub in Devon and one of the highest in the country. It stands at the side of the long moorland road between Two Bridges and Moretonhampstead.

INDEX

PLEASE HELP US BRING FRITH'S PHOTOGRAPHS TO LIFE

Our authors do their best to recount the history of the places they write about. They give insights into how particular towns and villages developed, they describe the architecture of streets and buildings, and they discuss the lives of famous people who lived there. But however knowledgeable our authors are, the story they tell is necessarily incomplete.

Frith's photographs are so much more than plain historical documents. They are living proofs of the flow of human life down the generations. They show real people at real moments in history; and each of those people is the son or daughter of someone, the brother or sister, aunt or uncle, grandfather or grandmother of someone else. All of them lived, worked and played in the streets depicted in Frith's photographs.

We would be grateful if you would tell us about the many places shown in our photographs—the streets with their buildings, shops, businesses and industries. Describe your own memories of life in those streets: what it was like growing up there, who ran the local shop and what shopping was like years ago; if your workplace is shown tell us about your working day and what the building is used for now. With your help more and more Frith photographs can be brought to life, and vital memories preserved for posterity.

We will gradually add your comments and stories to the archive for the benefit of historians of the future. Wherever possible, we will try to include some of your comments in future editions of our books. Moreover, if you spot errors in dates, titles or other facts, please let us know, because our archive records are not always completely accurate—they rely on 150 years of human endeavour and hand-compiled records.

So please write, fax or email us with your stories and memories. Thank you!

CHOOSE ANY PHOTOGRAPH FROM THIS BOOK

for your FREE Mounted Print. Order further prints at half price

Fill in and cut out the voucher on the next page and return it with your remittance for £2.50 for postage, packing and handling to UK addresses (US $5.00 for USA and Canada). For all other overseas addresses include £5.00 post and handling.
Choose any photograph included in this book. Make sure you quote its unique reference number eg. 42365 (it is mentioned after the photograph date. 1890 / 42365). Your SEPIA print will be approx 12" x 8" and mounted in a cream mount with a burgundy rule line (overall size 14" x 11").

Mounted Print
Overall size 14 x 11 inches

Order additional Mounted Prints at HALF PRICE - If you would like to order more Frith prints from this book, possibly as gifts for friends and family, you can buy them at half price (with no extra postage and handling costs) - only £7.49 each (UK orders), US $14.99 each (USA and Canada).

---

* IMPORTANT!

These special prices are only available if you order at the same time as you order your free mounted print. You must use the ORIGINAL VOUCHER on the facing page (no copies permitted). We can only despatch to one address.

Have your Mounted Prints framed (UK orders only) - For an extra £14.95 per print you can have your mounted print(s) framed in an elegant polished wood and gilt moulding, overall size 16" x 13" (no additional postage).

FRITH PRODUCTS AND SERVICES

All Frith photographs are available for you to buy as framed or mounted prints. From time to time, other illustrated items such as Address Books, Calendars, Table Mats are also available. Already, almost 50,000 Frith archive photographs can be viewed and purchased on the internet through the Frith website.

For more detailed information on Frith companies and products, visit

www.francisfrith.co.uk

For further information, trade, or author enquiries, contact:

The Francis Frith Collection, Frith's Barn, Teffont, Salisbury SP3 5QP
Tel: +44 (0) 1722 716 376 Fax: +44 (0) 1722 716 881 Email: sales@francisfrith.co.uk

Voucher for FREE and Reduced Price Frith Prints

Do not photocopy this voucher. Only the original is valid, so please fill it in, cut it out and return it to us with your order.

Picture ref no	Page number	Qty	Mounted @ £7.49 UK @$14.99 US	Framed + £14.95 (UK only)	US orders Total $	UK orders Total £
1		1	Free of charge*	£	$	£
2			£7.49 ($14.99)	£	$	£
3			£7.49 ($14.99)	£	$	£
4			£7.49 ($14.99)	£	$	£
5			£7.49 ($14.99)	£	$	£
			£7.49 ($14.99)	£	$	£
Please allow 28 days for delivery			* Post & handling		$5.00	£2.50
			Total Order Cost US $			£

Title of this book . . . .

I enclose a cheque / postal order (UK) for £ . . . . $ . . . .
payable to 'Francis Frith Collection' (USA orders 'Frith USA Inc')

OR debit my Mastercard / Visa / Switch (UK) / Amex card / Discover (USA)
(credit cards only on non UK and US orders), card details below

Card Number

Issue No (Switch only)   Valid from (Amex/Switch)

Expires   Signature

Name Mr/Mrs/Ms . . . .

Address . . . .

. . . .

. . . .

Postcode/Zip. . . . . Country . . . .

Daytime Tel No . . . .   Valid to 31/12/06

PAYMENT CURRENCY: We only accept payment in £ Sterling or US $.
If you are ordering **from any country, please pay by credit
card**, and you will be charged in one of these currencies.